MACHINES ★ AT WORK

TOW TRUCKS

BY CYNTHIA ROBERTS

THE CHILD'S WORLD® • MANKATO, MINNESOTA

The Child's World®

Published in the United States of America by The Child's World®
1980 Lookout Drive • Mankato, MN 56003-1705
800-599-READ • www.childsworld.com

PHOTO CREDITS
© Alan Schein Photography/Corbis: 20
© Corbis: 16
© David M. Budd Photography: cover, 2, 4, 7, 8, 11 (main), 12
© Gari Wyn Williams/Alamy: 11 (inset)
© Gunter Marx Photography/Corbis: 19
© iStockphoto.com/Simon Moran: 3
© Kim Karpeles/Alamy: 15

ACKNOWLEDGMENTS
The Child's World®: Mary Berendes, Publishing Director;
Katherine Stevenson, Editor

The Design Lab: Kathleen Petelinsek, Design and Page Production

LIBRARY OF CONGRESS CATALOGING-IN-PUBLICATION DATA
Roberts, Cynthia, 1960–
 Tow trucks / by Cynthia Roberts.
   p. cm. — (Machines at work)
 Includes bibliographical references and index.
 ISBN 1-59296-836-8 (library bound : alk. paper)
 1. Tow trucks—Juvenile literature. I. Title. II. Series.
 TL230.15.R64 2007
 629.225—dc22   2006023300

 Contents

This big tow truck is ready for its next job.

What are tow trucks?

Tow trucks are special kinds of **vehicles**. They pull or carry other vehicles. They are specially made for this job.

How are tow trucks used?

Tow trucks pull vehicles that cannot move on their own. Sometimes cars and trucks get in crashes. Sometimes they break down and will not run. Tow trucks take cars and trucks to places where people can fix them.

This tow truck is going to pull a fire truck. The fire truck needs to be fixed.

This tow truck has a big, roomy cab. Buttons and switches help the driver run the truck's towing parts. A radio lets him talk to other people.

What are the parts of a tow truck?

In the front, a tow truck looks like other trucks. It has a **cab** for the driver. The back of the truck looks different. It has special parts for towing other vehicles. These parts get their power from the truck's **engine**. The engine's power moves the truck, too.

Many tow trucks have a large arm on the back. The arm is called a **boom**. The end of the boom sometimes has a hook. The hook is on a long cable. A **winch** winds the cable and raises the hook.

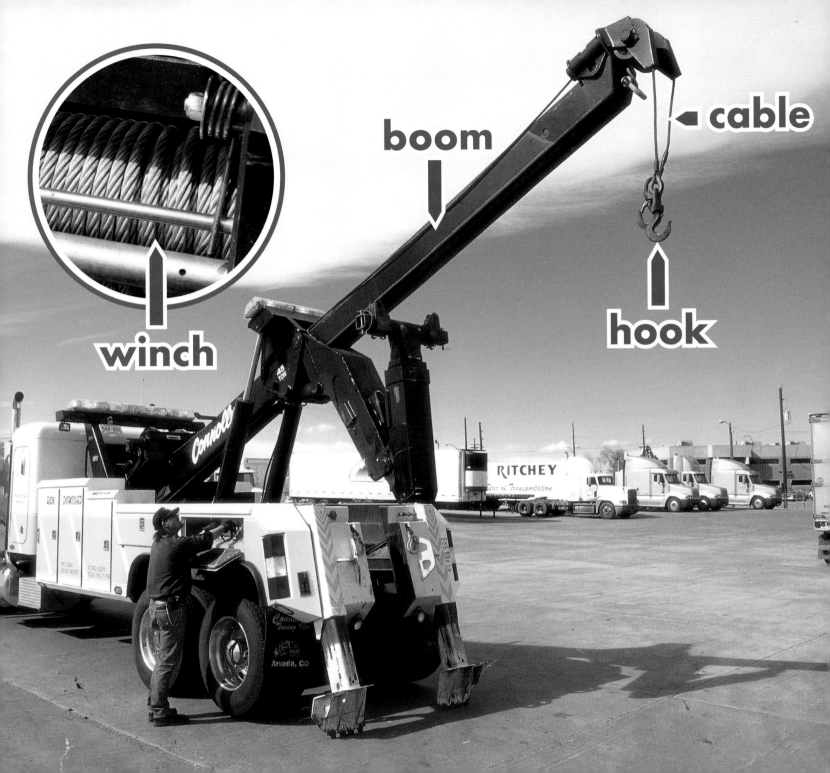

winch

boom

cable

hook

tow bar

This big, heavy tow bar is made of metal. ⭐
It is strong enough to lift other vehicles.

How do tow trucks tow?

Many tow trucks use a tow bar. The tow bar goes under one end of the vehicle. The tow truck raises the tow bar. Only two of the vehicle's wheels stay on the ground. The tow truck pulls the vehicle easily.

Many tow trucks use wheel lifts. The lifts go under the front or back wheels. The tow truck raises the wheel lifts. Then it pulls the vehicle along.

wheel lift

This driver is chaining a van to the wheel lift. The chains will keep the van from falling off.

This vehicle is being loaded onto a flatbed truck. The cable pulls it slowly into place.

Some tow trucks carry vehicles instead of towing them. They are called **flatbed** tow trucks.

Do tow trucks come in different sizes?

Tow trucks come in several sizes. Small ones can tow cars and small trucks. Large ones can tow big trucks and buses.

This tow truck is pulling a bus that crashed in Canada.

This tow truck has picked up a car in New York City.

Are tow trucks useful?

Tow trucks are used all over the world. They lift and pull heavy loads. They keep our roads safer. They save lots of time and hard work. Tow trucks are very useful!

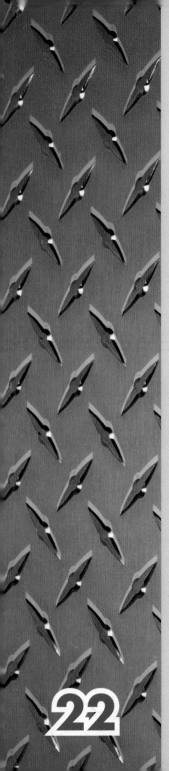

Glossary

boom (BOOM) A boom is long arm that holds something up.

cab (KAB) A machine's cab is the place where the driver sits.

engine (EN-jun) An engine is a machine that makes something move.

flatbed (FLAT-bed) Flatbed trucks or trailers have a big, flat body for carrying things.

vehicles (VEE-uh-kullz) Vehicles are things that carry people or goods.

winch (WINCH) A winch is a machine that raises or pulls things by winding a cable.

 # Books

Pomerantz, Charlotte, and R. W. Alley (illustrator). *How Many Trucks Can a Tow Truck Tow?* New York: Random House, 1997.

Teitelbaum, Michael. *If I Could Drive a Tow Truck.* New York: Scholastic, 2003.

 # Web Sites

Visit our Web site for lots of links about tow trucks:
http://www.childsworld.com/links
Note to parents, teachers, and librarians: We routinely check our Web links to make sure they're safe, active sites—so encourage your readers to check them out!

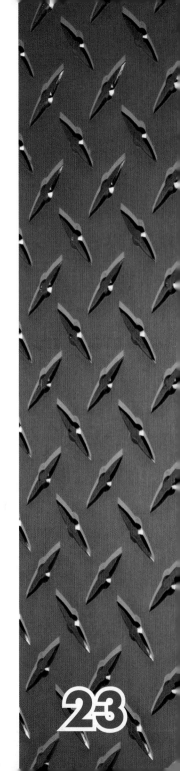

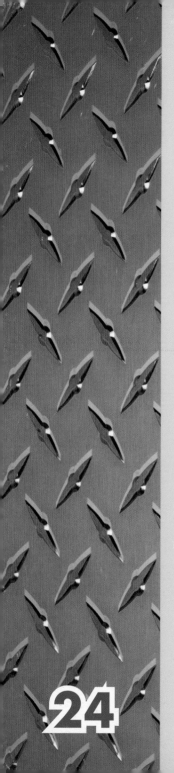

 # Index

 # About the Author

Even as a child, Cynthia Roberts knew she wanted to be a writer. She is always working to involve kids in reading and writing, and she loves spending time in the children's section of the library or bookstore. Cynthia enjoys gardening, traveling, and having fun with friends and family.